Seasons

Contents

Spring 2
Summer 4
Autumn 6
Winter 8
Seasons 10
Index 12

What can you see
in spring?

What can you see in summer?

What can you see in autumn?

What can you see
in winter?

Spring

Summer

Autumn

Winter

Index

autumn 6, 11

spring 2, 10

summer 4, 10

winter 8, 11